I AM ME
FROM A TO Z

Angelica R. Clark

Mindful Impressions, LLC
Mindfulimpressionsllc.com

Illustrations By Tooba Imtiaz

I Am Me: From A to Z

Copyright © 2022 by Angelica R. Clark

All rights reserved. Neither this book, nor any parts within it may be sold or reproduced in any form or by any electronic or mechanical means, including information storage and retrieval systems without permission in writing from the author.

The only exception is by a reviewer, who may quote short excerpts in a review.

Published by Mindful Impressions, LLC, in Sterlington, Louisiana

GET IN TOUCH
hello@mindfulimpressionsllc.com

LEARN MORE
www.mindfulimpressionsllc.com

ISBN (Paperback): 9781735816920
ISBN (eBook): 9781735816937
LCCN: 2022914372

Author's Note

"I Am" are two of the most powerful words you will ever speak. What you say after "I Am" will shape your future self and who you truly are, unapologetically.

Affirm your life with intention and watch the magic unfold before your beautiful eyes.

I Am: Awesome

I am Awesome because I am smart and kind, and I play well with others.

I think it is EVERYTHING about me that makes me so Awesome.

I Am: Brave

I am Brave because I have fears and I face them.

Being Brave may mean something different to others. Be your own Brave, and help others be their own Brave.

I Am: Encouraging

I am Encouraging because I give my friends the support they need to be themselves.

I am always Encouraging my friends to become their BEST selves because it Encourages me to do my best.

I Am: Gentle
I am Gentle with myself and others.

We are all doing the best we can with the knowledge and understanding we have. That is why it is always important to be Gentle.

I Am: Improving

Every day that I try, I am Improving myself.

Sometimes I may be fast and sometimes I may be slow, but I will always be happy with Improving myself.

I Am: Joyful

I make others around me happy because I am Joyful!

When I am Joyful, I make others around me Joyful.

I Am: Loved

I am Loved enough to share love and never run out.

I am Loved because my friends
and family accept me for who I am.

I Am: Me!

I am who I am meant to be.
I am who I want to be. I am who I choose to be. I Am Me!

Use the space below to illustrate yourself and your story.

I Am: Necessary

I was born with the Necessary tools to be an amazing person.

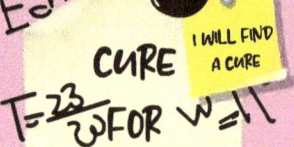
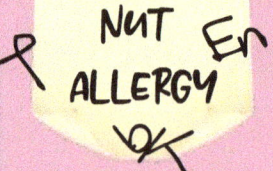

My journey from a child to an adult is a Necessary step to make the world a better place.

I Am: Outstanding

My creativity makes me Outstanding!

I am here to stand out and share my talents and gifts with the world.

I Am: Powerful

I believe I can do everything I set my mind to, and that makes me Powerful.

I WILL BE SUCCESSFUL.

I WILL MAKE GOOD GRADES.

I WILL CREATE A BRIGHT FUTURE FOR MYSELF.

I am most Powerful when I am my true, authentic self.

I Am: Relentless

I am Relentless in the belief that I can become whomever I choose to become.

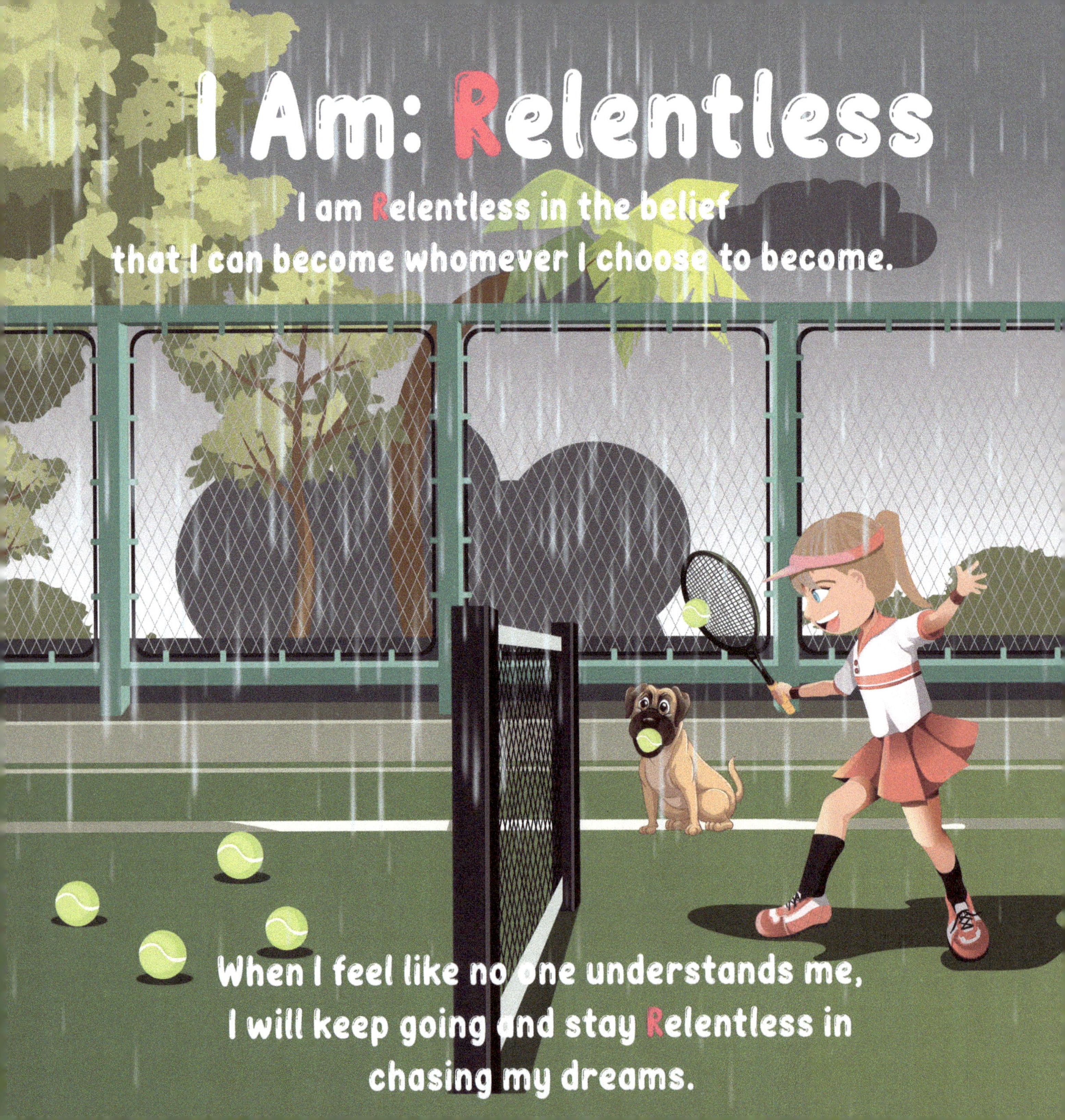

When I feel like no one understands me, I will keep going and stay Relentless in chasing my dreams.

I Am: Successful

I am Successful in everything
I do because I was born to do so.

It doesn't matter if I win or lose.
Success is my birthright, and all I have to do is try.

I Am: Thoughtful

I am Thoughtful about and sensitive to the feelings and needs of others.

I am always Thoughtful about what I do and say to my friends, to my family, and most importantly, to myself.

I Am: Unique

I am Unique, and I shine in my own special way.

No one will ever be me, and that is what makes me so Unique. I love being me!

I Am: Valuable

I am Valuable not because of what I do or say, but simply because I am alive and happy.

My Value does not decrease because I made a mistake. Win or lose, I am Valuable, and I matter!

I Am: Whole

I am Whole and complete because I have
family and friends that love me for me.

I have everything I need to become my
very best self, and that makes me Whole.

I Am: eXceptional

I am the eXceptional result of being loved by eXceptional people that I call family.

My superpower is my ability to think differently than others, and that makes me eXceptional.

I Am: Zen

Take a deep breath in, hold it for five seconds, and let it out.

Take another deep breath in, hold it for five seconds, and let it out.

Take one last deep breath in, hold it for five seconds, and let it out.

Quietly say to yourself...

I Am Me!

And that is enough.

And So It Is!

Color Me!

What's my name? _____

Share me on social media and tag @mindfulimpressionsllc to be featured on their page!

www.ingramcontent.com/pod-product-compliance
Lightning Source LLC
Chambersburg PA
CBHW051322110526
44590CB00031B/4438